Essential Question
How are kids around the world different?

Sharing Cultures

by Christopher Herrera
illustrated by Laura Jacobsen

Mrs. Gupta's class is surprised.
What does she have on?

"Good morning, class! Today
we will learn about each
other's **customs**. I'll go first,"
says Mrs. Gupta.

sari

dosa

She says, "This is a sari. My family is from India. Many women wear saris there. Indians also eat these rice pancakes."

STOP AND CHECK

What are some Indian customs?

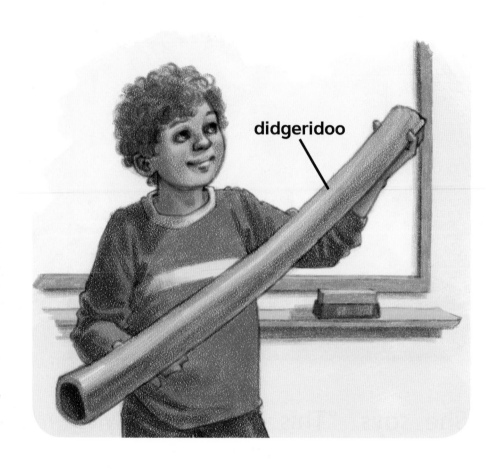

didgeridoo

The next day Darel starts. "My family is from Australia. People play this instrument there."

The class **wonders** how it is played. Darrel shows them.

"That's cool!" thinks Alex. "But I don't have an instrument to share."

daruma

Akita says, "I am from Japan. We give these dolls at New Year."

6

"You color in one eye," Akita says. "Then make a **wish**. **Suppose** it comes true. Then color in the other eye."

"Akita has given me an idea!" thinks Alex.

STOP AND CHECK

What are some customs in Australia and Japan?

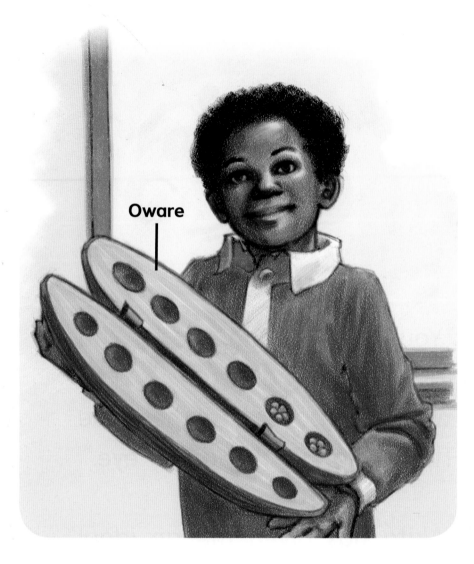

Oware

Awo says, "I am from Ghana, Africa. We play a game with stones. This is the wooden board."

Awo says, "You pick up the stones. You must do it in **order**."

"My father is from Russia," says Anton. "They have snow in winter there. The trees in the park are **brightly** lit. Children go sledding."

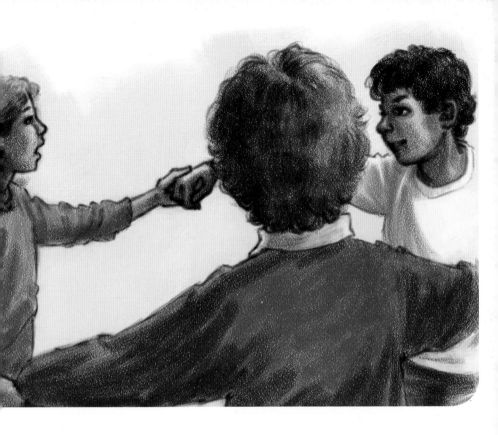

"Some people dance for
the **crowd**," says Anton. He
shows how to do the dance.

STOP AND CHECK

What are some customs
in Ghana and Russia?

11

Benita is **dressed** like a **mermaid**.
She says, "My mother is from
Brazil. Carnival is a **favorite**
holiday there."

"We went to Carnival last year. People dressed up," Benita says. "They walked through the city."

At last, it is Alex's turn.

"I am Native American," says Alex. "This is a storyteller doll. The doll has many children. They listen to her stories. Stories are how we pass on our customs. Just like we are doing now!"

storyteller doll

STOP AND CHECK

What is a custom that Akita and Alex share?

15

Respond to Reading

Summarize

Summarize *Sharing Cultures*. The chart may help you.

	Russia	Brazil
holiday		
custom		

Text Evidence

1. How are the customs in the story alike? Compare and Contrast

2. Turn to page 14. What does the word *pass* mean here?

   Vocabulary

3. Write about two customs in the story. Tell how they are alike and different.

   Write About Reading

Compare Texts
What are customs in different parts of the world?

Music Around the World

Darel shared an instrument from Australia. Let's look at some other instruments.

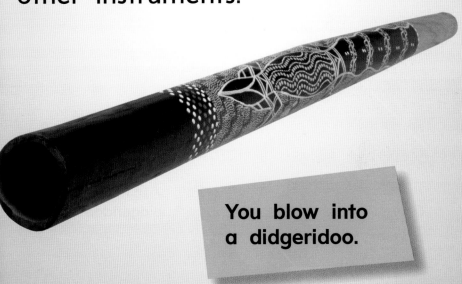

You blow into a didgeridoo.

This is a thumb piano. It comes from Africa. To play it, you hold the wooden box. You pluck the keys with your thumbs.

A thumb piano is called an mbira.

Trinidad and Tobago
steelpans

Australia
didgeridoo

Africa
thumb piano

This is a steelpan. It is a kind of drum from Trinidad and Tobago. You hit the steelpan with sticks to play it.

Steelpans are made from steel drums.

Make Connections

How can kids in different countries play music? Essential Question

Look at both texts. What are two customs in Africa? Text to Text

Focus on
Literary Elements

Characters Characters are the people in a story.

What to Look for Look at what the characters say in *Sharing Cultures.* Look at what they do. This shows what they are like.

Your Turn

Describe Benita. What does she say? What does she look like? What does she do?